Antonio VIVALDI

(1678 – 1741)

Concerto for Cello and Orchestra, RV 399
C Major / Ut majeur / C-Dur

Edited by
Josef Hofer

DOWANI International

Preface

Of the 26 cello concertos listed in the catalogue of Vivaldi's work (the Ryom Verzeichnis), the concerto for cello and orchestra RV 399 in C Major is amongst the most popular. The reason for its popularity may lie in the Venetian Baroque master's typical style of composition. It may also however be due to the fact that the piece is technically easy to play. The solo part can be played entirely in first position, which makes it a very suitable teaching piece, and a good introduction to original pieces of music from this period. A few changes of position are given as options, which allow the piece to be played in different and more contemporary sounding ways. The player must himself decide which way he or she would like to perform it. Our edition enables you to learn this piece systematically and in three varying tempi with professional accompaniments.

The CD opens with the concert version of each movement (cello and orchestra). After tuning your instrument (Track 1), the musical work can begin. Your first practice session should be at slow tempo. If your stereo system is equipped with a balance control, you can place either the cello or the piano accompaniment in the foreground by adjusting the control. The cello always remains softly audible in the background as a guide. In the middle position, both instruments can be heard at the same volume. If you do not have a balance control, you can listen to the solo part on one loudspeaker and the piano part on the other. Having mastered the slow tempo, you can now advance to the medium and original tempos. The piano or orchestral accompaniment can be heard on both channels (without cello) in stereo quality. Each movement has been sensibly divided into subsections for practice purposes. You can select the subsection you want using the track numbers indicated in the solo part. Further explanations can be found at the end of this volume along with the names of the musicians involved in the recording. More detailed information can be found in the Internet at www.dowani.com. All of the versions were recorded live.

The fingering and bowing marks in this edition were provided by Josef Hofer, a cellist and teacher living in Liechtenstein. Hofer studied with Walter Grimmer in Berne and Gerhard Mantel in Frankfurt am Main. He is well known as a chamber musician and jury member at various national and international competitions and has taught for many years in Liechtenstein and Switzerland. He is also the author of the *Kompendien für Cello*, published by DOWANI (order numbers: DOW 3701-3715), a German language cello tutor, which is becoming ever more popular amongst cello teachers. Details can be found on the Internet under: www.dowani.com.

We wish you lots of fun playing from our *DOWANI 3 Tempi Play Along* editions and hope that your musicality and diligence will enable you to play the concert version as soon as possible. Our goal is to provide the essential conditions you need for effective practicing through motivation, enjoyment and fun.

Your DOWANI Team

Avant-propos

Le concerto RV 399 en Ut majeur est un des plus populaires parmi les 26 concertos pour violoncelle répertoriés dans le catalogue des œuvres d'Antonio Vivaldi (catalogue Ryom). Cela est probablement dû, d'une part, à l'écriture typique du maître vénitien, et d'autre part à la facilité technique relative de cette composition. La partie soliste peut être jouée presque entièrement dans la première position, constituant ainsi un morceau de choix pour l'enseignement et une première approche de la musique de cette époque. Afin de faciliter une interprétation différentiée, quelques changements de position ont été indiqués en option. Mais l'interprète est invité de choisir lui-même sa manière d'exécuter. Notre édition vous propose d'étudier cette œuvre de manière systématique dans trois tempos différents avec un accompagnement professionnel.

Le CD vous permettra d'entendre d'abord la version de concert de chaque mouvement (violoncelle et orchestre). Après avoir accordé votre instrument (plage n° 1), vous pourrez commencer le travail musical. Votre premier contact avec le morceau devrait se faire à un tempo lent. Si votre chaîne hi-fi dispose d'un réglage de balance, vous pouvez l'utiliser pour mettre au premier plan soit le violoncelle, soit l'accompagnement de piano. Le violoncelle restera cependant toujours très doucement à l'arrière-plan comme point de repère. En équilibrant la balance, vous entendrez les deux instruments à volume égal. Si vous ne disposez pas de réglage de balance, vous entendrez l'instrument soliste sur un des haut-parleurs et le piano sur l'autre. Après avoir étudié le morceau à un tempo lent, vous pourrez ensuite travailler à un tempo modéré et au tempo original. Dans ces deux tempos vous entendrez l'ac-compagnement de piano ou d'orchestre sur les deux canaux en stéréo (sans la partie soliste). Chaque mouvement a été divisé en sections judicieuses pour faciliter le travail. Vous pouvez sélectionner ces sections à l'aide des numéros de plages indiqués dans la partie du soliste. Pour obtenir plus d'informations et les noms des artistes qui ont participé aux enregistrements, veuillez consulter la dernière page de cette édition ou notre site Internet : www.dowani.com. Toutes les versions ont été enregistrées en direct.

Les doigtés et indications des coups d'archet proviennent du violoncelliste et pédagogue Josef Hofer qui vit au Liechtenstein. Il étudia auprès de Walter Grimmer à Berne et Gerhard Mantel à Francfort-sur-le-Main. Josef Hofer est musicien de chambre et membre de jury de divers concours nationaux et internationaux. Il enseigne depuis de nombreuses années au Liechtenstein et en Suisse. Il a, par ailleurs, compilé les *Compendia pour violoncelle*, ouvrages pédagogiques parus chez DOWANI (réf. DOW 3701 à 3715) rencontrant un succès grandissant auprès des professeurs de violoncelle. Vous trouverez des informations détaillées concernant les *Compendia* sur Internet à l'adresse www.dowani.com.

Nous vous souhaitons beaucoup de plaisir à faire de la musique avec la collection *DOWANI 3 Tempi Play Along* et nous espérons que votre musicalité et votre application vous amèneront aussi rapidement que possible à la version de concert. Notre but est de vous offrir les bases nécessaires pour un travail efficace par la motivation et le plaisir.

Les Éditions DOWANI

Vorwort

Von den 26 Cellokonzerten, die im Verzeichnis der Werke Antonio Vivaldis (Ryom-Verzeichnis) aufgeführt sind, zählt das Konzert für Violoncello und Orchester RV 399 in C-Dur zu den beliebtesten. Das mag zum einen an der typischen Kompositionsweise des venezianischen Barockmeisters liegen, zum anderen aber auch an der leichten technischen Spielbarkeit. Der Solopart kann durchwegs in der 1. Lage ausgeführt werden und eignet sich somit bestens als Unterrichtsliteratur und als erster Kontakt zu einem Originalwerk aus dieser Epoche. Für eine differenzierte und klanglich zeitgemäße Darstellung wurden ergänzend einige Lagenwechsel als Option angegeben. Es ist aber dem Spieler selbst überlassen, für welche Ausführungsart er sich entscheidet. Unsere Ausgabe ermöglicht es Ihnen, das Werk systematisch und in drei verschiedenen Tempi mit professioneller Begleitung zu erarbeiten.

Auf der CD können Sie zuerst die Konzertversion (Cello mit Orchester) eines jeden Satzes anhören. Nach dem Stimmen Ihres Instrumentes (Track 1) kann die musikalische Arbeit beginnen. Ihr erster Übe-Kontakt mit dem Stück sollte im langsamen Tempo stattfinden. Wenn Ihre Stereoanlage über einen Balance-Regler verfügt, können Sie durch Drehen des Reglers entweder das Cello oder die Klavierbegleitung stufenlos in den Vordergrund blenden. Das Cello bleibt jedoch immer als Orientierungshilfe – wenn auch sehr leise – hörbar. In der Mittelposition erklingen beide Instrumente gleich laut. Falls Sie keinen Balance-Regler haben, hören Sie das Soloinstrument auf dem einen Lautsprecher, das Klavier auf dem anderen. Nachdem Sie das Stück im langsamen Tempo einstudiert haben, können Sie im mittelschnellen und originalen Tempo musizieren. Die Klavier- bzw. Orchesterbegleitung erklingt hierbei auf beiden Kanälen (ohne Cello) in Stereo-Qualität. Jeder Satz wurde in sinnvolle Übe-Abschnitte unterteilt. Diese können Sie mit Hilfe der in der Solostimme angegebenen Track-Nummern auswählen. Weitere Erklärungen hierzu sowie die Namen der Künstler finden Sie auf der letzten Seite dieser Ausgabe; ausführlichere Informationen können Sie im Internet unter www.dowani.com nachlesen. Alle eingespielten Versionen wurden live aufgenommen.

Die Fingersätze und Striche in dieser Ausgabe stammen von dem in Liechtenstein lebenden Cellisten und Pädagogen Josef Hofer. Er studierte bei Walter Grimmer in Bern sowie bei Gerhard Mantel in Frankfurt am Main. Josef Hofer ist als Kammermusiker und Jurymitglied bei diversen nationalen und internationalen Wettbewerben tätig und unterrichtet seit vielen Jahren in Liechtenstein und der Schweiz. Er ist außerdem Autor der bei DOWANI erschienenen *Kompendien für Cello* (Bestellnummer: DOW 3701-3715), einem Lehrwerk, das sich bei den Cellolehrern immer größerer Beliebtheit erfreut. Detaillierte Informationen zu den *Kompendien* finden Sie im Internet unter: www.dowani.com/kompendium.

Wir wünschen Ihnen viel Spaß beim Musizieren mit unseren *DOWANI 3 Tempi Play Along*-Ausgaben und hoffen, dass Ihre Musikalität und Ihr Fleiß Sie möglichst bald bis zur Konzertversion führen werden. Unser Ziel ist es, Ihnen durch Motivation, Freude und Spaß die notwendigen Voraussetzungen für effektives Üben zu schaffen.

Ihr DOWANI Team

Concerto

for Cello and Orchestra, RV 399

C Major / Ut majeur / C-Dur

A. Vivaldi (1678 – 1741)
Piano Reduction: G. Stöver

DOW 3507

Cello

Concerto

for Cello and Orchestra, RV 399
C Major / Ut majeur / C-Dur

A. Vivaldi (1678 – 1741)
Edited by J. Hofer

DOW 3507